Advanced Knitting Mastery

KNITTING TRICKS, TIPS & TECHNIQUES

By

Karen Doyle

Published by:

CSBA Publishing

CSBA Publishing House

Cover & Interior designed

By

Heather Ross

First Edition

TABLE OF CONTENTS

INTRODUCTION

So, you've got your basics down, and your friends are getting a little sick of having to model the same scarf over and over. It's time to take your knitwear to the next level! Once you are comfortable with the fundamentals of construction, you can start to get stylish with your stitches and patterns.

In this guide, I will address some of the most common intermediate to advanced techniques that will elevate your projects from labors of love to gorgeous garments.

We will look carefully at the stitch level in order to understand the building blocks of knitwear, and hopefully, by the time we are done, you will be inspired to create your own designs. One of the best things about knitting is that the possibilities are practically endless-- it's all up to you!

Let's get started, shall we?

ESSENTIAL TOOLS YOU WILL NEED

CABLE NEEDLES

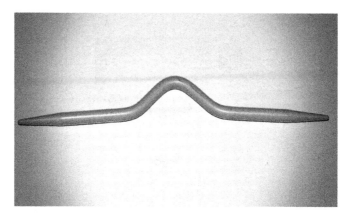

Cable needles are double pointed needles with a dip in the middle, used for holding stitches to the front or back of the work as a cable is formed. They come in standard needle sizes and, because of their double pointed nature, stitches can be worked directly from the needle as opposed to a regular stitch holder.

Although cable needles are not required for working cable patterns, they can make your life much easier if you are working a cable-heavy piece.

Essential to working in the round or any project involving pattern repeats, stitch markers make your life as a knitter that much easier. My favorite versions have a safety pin-style closure that allows you to add or remove them at any time while being a bit more secure than their split ring cousins.

Specially designated markers are, however, completely unnecessary-- you can use anything from paper clips to scrap yarn to mark your place, as long as it can fit over your needle!

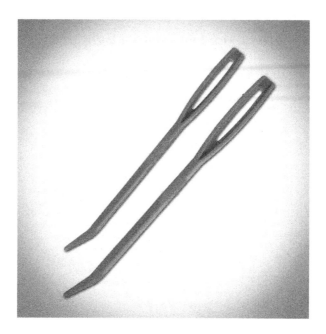

Tapestry needles are much larger than sewing needles and often are made of plastic. Also known as yarn needles, they are used for finishing work, such as grafting and weaving in loose ends. Their blunt points are designed to pass through existing holes rather than create them, therefore protecting the integrity of the yarn by separating as few fibers as possible.

They come in many different sizes, and when choosing a yarn needle just make sure it has an eye that is wide enough to accommodate your project yarn. Bent tip needles have a slight bend towards the point of the needle that makes it possible to grab stitches one at a time without having to pull them up, leading to a tighter, neater finished product.

POINT PROTECTORS

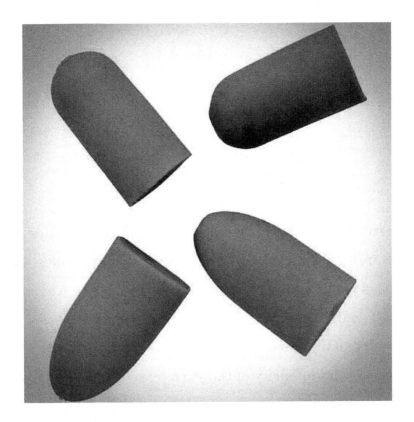

Does exactly what it says on the tin-- a little rubber cap that fits over the pointed part of your needle. These both prevent stitches from sliding off and keep safe objects your needles might otherwise poke.

They come in single and double versions, for holding circular needles together, and are particularly useful for transporting works in progress.

PART -1

ADVANCED TECHNIQUES

A FEW ADVANCED TECHNIQUES YOU MUST LEARN

WORKING IN THE ROUND

Working in the round is a valuable and versatile skill to add to your repertoire. Hats, socks, mittens, sleeves...the project list goes on and on. This technique creates a seamless tube of fabric instead of a flat piece. If you have never worked in the round before, there are a couple of things to keep in mind. Stitch patterns will be slightly different from flat knitting because the work is never turned.

For example, stockinette stitch in the round is worked via continuous knit rows, no purling involved. Casting on over circular or double pointed needles is exactly the same as straight needles, and the round is created only by joining your working yarn to the first cast on stitch by knitting (or purling, depending on your pattern).

It is essential to make sure your cast on row is not twisted when you first join your rounds, or your whole project will follow! All of these concepts will soon become second nature as you work them for yourself and gain experience in circular projects.

DPNs (Double Pointed Needles)

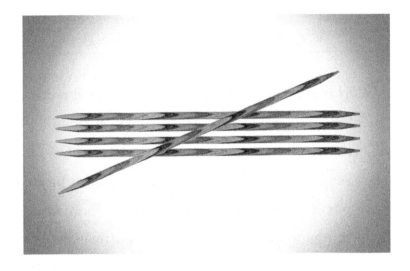

Don't run away just yet! Not nearly as frightening as they look, double pointed needles are one of the best ways to expand your knitting skills beyond the world of scarves (your friends will thank you!). Unlike a traditional knitting needle, double pointed needles taper at both ends, allowing stitches to be knit from either direction. The total number of stitches for your project will be evenly divided between multiple needles, with the stitches on only one needle being worked at a time.

They are usually sold in sets of five, with three or four needles being used to hold the work while one is used to knit. Traditionally three needles are used, forming a triangle shape that lends itself naturally to working in the round, but using four can be helpful if your pattern increases or decreases in a multiple of four or if all of your stitches cannot fit on three needles.

Although they look torturous and complicated, double pointed needles are no more difficult to use than regular needles!

CIRCULAR NEEDLES

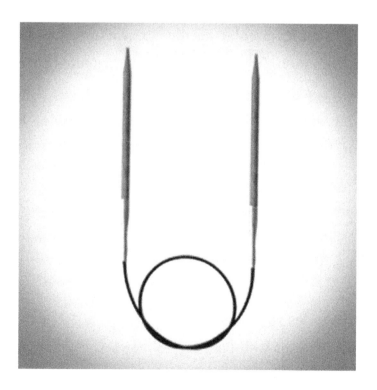

One of the great modern marvels of the knitting world! If you have forayed into hat making at all, it's likely that you have already experienced the 16" circular needle. These simple tools are a game changer for your repertoire. Circular needles are two short needles attached by a plastic cord, though they come in just as many material varieties as straight needles. There are even interchangeable sets, which allow different sized needles to be screwed on to different lengths of cords, giving you maximum customizability.

Many people find circular needles to be a more comfortable (and less anxiety-inducing) alternative to double pointed needles. They also allow you to create a seamless tube of fabric, but often on a larger scale, and their varying lengths (up to 40"!) mean they are excellent for holding a sizable amount of stitches. When working in the round and deciding which needles to use, it is important to remember that the circumference of your project can only be as small as the length of your needle.

The 36" needles you used to hold your 300 stitch shawl will likely not work as well for your 18" cowl. Circular projects will be joined in the round and then knit continuously. Projects to be worked flat proceed as they would on straight needles, turning the work each time you finish a row.

MAGIC LOOP

If you're not entirely comfortable with the idea of all those double points hanging out waiting to drop a stitch, or you can't quite justify dropping cash on a whole new set of needles just to finish your hat, then the "magic loop" method will be perfect for you. This is an informal technique that lets you use circular needles to knit things much smaller than their circumference.

It is not recommended that you use this for the entirety of small projects such as gloves and socks (if only because readjusting your needles every ten stitches or so can become annoying very quickly), but it is a neat fix for working decreases under 16". Using a long circular needle, preferably 24" and up, cast on your project stitches.

Now find the midpoint and gently pull the cable between the stitches, sliding the stitches to the needle points. Make sure your edge is not twisted (!) and transfer the last stitch you cast on to the other needle.

Slipping this stitch will ensure a tidy join along the cast-on edge, but it is not necessary. It is, however, now the first stitch of your round, so make sure to place a marker if needed. Pull the right-hand needle out of the stitches, leaving a couple of inches of cord slack, and let them rest on the cable. Knit with this needle as you would normally in your pattern.

You will see two loops formed by the cable on either side of your work! When you have finished working the half of the stitches that were on your left needle, pull the cord of the loop that remains until your stitches are back on both needle points. Pull the needle point from the worked stitches, making another loop, and use it to knit the other set.

That's it! Just keep shimmying your stitches around like this and knit as you would per your pattern. This technique is very intuitive once you put your hands to it.

Here is a video of Magic loop from YouTube

https://www.youtube.com/watch?v=ldSpc0EZpnk

PROVISIONAL CAST-ON

This temporary cast-on is great when you are starting a project somewhere other than the finished edge. It keeps your cast-on stitches "live" so that they may be knit from seamlessly or grafted to another piece at a later point.

This method works well for when you want to start the body of your project but aren't sure of specifics such as length or edging. It is also useful for directional patterns with a midpoint, perhaps a scarf with symmetrical color work, as it lets you pick up stitches and continue working without having to reverse your pattern.

Although there are "proper" methods to working this cast-on (some even involving crochet hooks!), there is a remarkably simple workaround that requires no new skills. Simply knit a couple of rows with a different colored scrap yarn and then switch to your project yarn. Almost too easy, right? When the time comes, you will be able to quickly unravel the two or three provisional rows and pick up your live stitches without a hitch!

INCREASES

Increases do exactly what they say-- these techniques add an additional stitch to your needle once they are completed. This is essential for shaping garments and can also be used in decorative stitching. In advanced knitting, it is important to become familiar with working through both the front and back of a stitch. It appears pretty straightforward when knitting, but when purling it can be less intuitive.

Knitting through the front loop

Knitting through the back loop

Purling through the front loop

Purling through the back loop

Make One (M1)

Definitely the most well-known increase technique. Technically it is called a Make One left (M1L) because the leading edge of the stitch you create will twist left. If you dig deep enough you can find Make One Right (M1R) designated in some patterns, however it is so uncommon that if a pattern simply calls for you to "make one" you will perform the following (Note: if you are purling and required to M1, the same steps will apply, but you will purl instead of knitting):

1. Find the horizontal bar between your two stitches

2. Pick it up with your left needle from front to back

3. Knit this bar through the back loop

4. You have increased by one! See how the stitch twists to the left?

To complete an M1R, you will lift the bar from behind and knit through its front loop. Go ahead and try both and see if you can begin to tell the difference!

BAR INCREASE

Another common increase technique, named for the little dash that follows each increased stitch. This bar is visible on the knit side of the fabric whether the increase is worked on the right or wrong side. It can be very attractive when evenly spaced!

1. Insert your right-hand needle as if to knit

2. Wrap your yarn and pull it through, as if to knit, but leave the stitch on the left needle

3. Insert your right needle into the back of the same stitch

4. Knit and slip the stitch off of the left needle

DECREASES

Decreases also do exactly what they say-- these techniques subtract a single stitch from your needle upon completion.

The different methods are all about how you want your finished piece to look.

"KNIT 2 TOGETHER" (K2TOG)

Creates a right leaning decrease.

1. Place your right-hand needle at the back of the second stitch on your left needle, as if to knit.

2. Slide your right-hand needle through both the second and first stitch and wrap your yarn around it, as if to knit.

3. Knit the two stitches together with your right-hand needle and slide them off the left-hand needle. See how the stitch points to the right?

SLIP, SLIP, KNIT (SSK)

Creates a left-leaning decrease.

Here are the six steps to SSK

1. Place your right-hand needle at the back of the first stitch on your left-hand needle, as if to knit.

2. Slip that stitch onto your right needle

3. Place your right-hand needle at the back of the next stitch on your left-hand needle, as if to knit.

4. Slip that stitch onto your right needle.

5. Slide your left-hand needle through both slipped stitches, with your right-hand needle in back.

6. Wrap your yarn around the right needle and knit the two together, sliding them off the right-hand needle. Now the stitch points left!

SHORT ROW SHAPING

Short rows, also known as partial or turning rows, are nothing more than extra rows knit to shape or curve a part of your garment. They are called short rows because you will only be working a certain chunk of stitches along your needle and will turn the work before you reach the end of the row ("partial" and "turning" rows, you get me?).

This is one of those elements that will really inform your structural understanding of knitwear garments and how they differ from sewn pieces. It is this kind of shaping that can elevate your basic pattern to a truly flattering end. It is a super easy concept, and the only trick you have to learn is how to prevent gaps from forming between the turned stitches and the rest of your row.

As it is for many knitting techniques, there are a few different methods that reach the same results. We will be looking at the wrap-and-turn, but I encourage you to explore other approaches and find out which one works best for you!

When you come to the end of your short row, a.k.a the turning point:

1. With the yarn in back, slip the next stitch purlwise

2. Bring the yarn to the front of the work

3. Slip the same stitch back to the left needle

4. Turn your work to begin your short row, bringing the
   yarn between the needles

Ta-da! That wrap will prevent a gap from forming between your short row and the rest of your knitting. The technique is much the same for when you are turning on a purl row (except for that you will start with your yarn in front before slipping the stitch and bring it to the back after).

As you go, you will see that the wrap-and-turn creates a noticeable tick in the continuity of your fabric. If you prefer to hide these wraps, when you have completed all of your short rows, take these following 4 steps.

1. Work to just before the wrapped stitch

2. Insert the needle under the wrap and then knitwise into the wrapped stitch

3. Knit the two together

Your turning points are now invisible! On a purled side, the method is much the same:

1. Work to just before the wrapped stitch

2. Insert the right needle from behind into the back loop of the wrap

3. Place the wrap on the left needle

4. Purl the lifted wrap and the wrapped stitch together

On purl rows, in particular, it can be a bit tricky to find your wrap. If you are having difficulty, try placing a marker on each of your wraps as you go to make sure you find them all at the end!

SELVAGES

Historically a weaving term for the finished edge of a fabric, selvage has made its way into the knitting vocabulary as much the same. Woven fabrics bind their own edges through the weaving process, as the horizontal weft fibers wrap around the vertical warp on the turn of the shuttle, giving rise to the term "self-edge."

Since the 16th century, this phrase has morphed into the word "selvage" as we know it. While knitted fabric does create its own edge (or else you'd be unravelling all over the place), you can add selvage stitches to a piece to stabilize the fabric or really give edges a finished look.

A selvage is usually only one or two stitches (but it can certainly be more), and these should be added to your total stitch count. As you well know by now, stockinette stitch curls with a fury. By adding a quick selvage, you can firm up the edges of your scarf and deter the inward roll.

The same can be said for openwork pieces that tend to widen, or when working with slippery fibers such as silk-- a selvage can help keep these pieces in shape. These extra stitches are also great for preparing pieces for seaming, as they can serve as a seam allowance that disappears when the pieces are sewn together. This can be particularly helpful in keeping your colorwork uninterrupted across a seamed piece.

What your selvage consists of is up to you-- it's all about what kind of purpose it will be serving. A simple fixed edge can be achieved through just a garter stitch (*K1, work the row to its last stitch, K1* repeat) on either side, but if you wanted something really sturdy you could work a few columns in seed stitch.

Although not particularly decorative, a slip stitch selvage is great for seaming and perfect for picking up stitches later.

1. (RS rows) Slip the first stitch knitwise, work to the last stitch, knit one
2. (WS rows) Slip the first stitch purlwise, work to the last stitch, purl one

Repeat these two rows, and you will see a chain stitch on either side of your piece. Each chain loop you end up making will be representative of two rows.

Garter stitch selvage

Slip stitch selvage

GRAFTING

The time will inevitably come when you find yourself with two rows of stitches that you must somehow fix together. Enter the Kitchener stitch. This technique allows you to seamlessly weave live stitches together. It can be a tad daunting when it is all written out, but the only tricky part is keeping track of where you are in the steps. You will see a sort of rhythm appear after the first couple of stitches, which makes it easy to do all in one shot.

Start with your stitches on two parallel needles, wrong sides facing each other. Thread your needle with your project yarn for a continuous result-- we're using red here for contrast!

1. Insert your needle into the first stitch on the front needle, as if to PURL. Pull the yarn through, leaving the stitch on the needle.

2. Insert the needle through the first stitch on the back needle, as if to KNIT. Pull the yarn through, leaving the stitch on the needle.

3. Insert the needle through the first stitch on the front needle, as if to KNIT. Pull the yarn through and slip the stitch off the needle.

4. Insert the needle through the new first stitch on the front needle, as if to PURL. Pull the yarn through, leaving the stitch on the needle.

5. Insert the needle through the first stitch on the back needle, as if to PURL. Pull the yarn through and slip the stitch off the needle.

5. Insert the needle through the new first stitch on the back needle, as if to KNIT. Pull the yarn through, leaving the stitch on the needle.

Repeat steps 3-6 until all necessary stitches have been worked. Make sure to check your tension every couple stitches or so-- you want your grafted row to blend seamlessly with the rest of the piece. Because there is no seam, this technique is essential for sock toes and other places in garments where a raised edge against the body can be irritating.

BLOCKING

Ever wonder why your projects never look quite as good as the ones in the pictures? You've followed the pattern meticulously, but your version still looks just a little sloppy somehow? About as boring as knitting a gauge swatch (but equally as important!), blocking is the final step in perfecting your finished pieces and getting that professional look.

Is that sweater you made just a little too lumpy to wear outside? Is one sleeve just a tad longer than the other? Before you secret it away in the attic and go back to making scarves forever, break out your ironing board and spray bottle and block that puppy into shape! Blocking turns your inevitably varied hand knits into beautifully even fabrics by gently stretching and redistributing stitches amongst the work.

This will not work miracles for egregiously mismatched pieces, but if you ever find yourself dismayed at how differently things knit up (even though you use the same hands and needles every time!), you will be surprised at how much consistency this technique will allow you to regain. Blocked pieces are much easier to work with due to the newfound uniformity of the fabric, and therefore the construction of projects like sweaters is often better left until after the individual pieces have been shaped.

If you have never blocked before, you will be truly amazed to find out how great of a knitter you actually are. It is an easy and uncomplicated way towards making your garments look and fit that much better!

Accessories You Will Need:

- Flat, padded surface large enough to hold your piece; Specialty blocking boards are convenient but not necessary. I often use my ironing board with a folded bath towel on top for smaller pieces, but you could even just lay a few layers of towels out on your kitchen table for something larger. Feel free to get creative-- as long as you are able to pin your piece flat and the surface doesn't mind getting hot or wet, you should be good to go.

- Rust-proof pins; T pins are the best for blocking because of their robust body and metal head. Make sure the pins you use are tall enough to go through your knitting without disappearing. Never use pins with plastic heads for steam blocking-- the last thing you want is gooey plastic melted into your piece and all over your iron.

- Water source; As long as you can fill it with water and your garment will be submerged completely, any kind of storage tub, large bowl, or even a clean sink can be used for wet blocking. A water-filled spray bottle is convenient for wetting your piece, but you can also use the spray function on your iron (just make sure the heat is off!).

Before you block, you must determine what kind of yarn you are working with. Natural and synthetic fibers have their own particular properties and will react differently to heat and moisture. Wool and wool-like fibers (alpaca, cashmere, camel, etc.) have a hooked structure that compels them to stick together (this is why they are considered the best fibers for felting).

They are porous and far more susceptible to softening and molding in water than plastics. Synthetic fibers (acrylics, rayons, nylons, etc.) require gentle heat in order to relax their rigid structure. Plant fibers such as cotton, linen, and bamboo can generally be blocked using either method.

WET BLOCKING

(Use with natural fibers, best for wools and the like)

Wet blocking can be done either by submerging your piece in lukewarm water, squeezing it out (gently!) and pinning it to a flat board or by pinning it first and spraying the piece with water until it is damp.

The piece should be pinned to the exact measurements of your pattern; stretch and push the fabric to reach your desired shape. Leave to dry COMPLETELY. This can often take over 24 hours, but any kind of finegaling that happens while the piece is still damp can affect the result of your block.

STEAM BLOCKING

(Best for synthetic fibers or blends)

Steam blocking uses the heat and moisture from an iron or steamer to set your stitches into place. Pin your piece to its desired dimensions first, then hover the iron/steamer over it until the fabric becomes damp, pushing the stitches into shape as you go.

Do not place the iron directly on your garment, as you can press the shape out of decorative stitching and even melt synthetic yarns! If you must press lightly (and only with natural fibers!), always place a colorfast cloth between your work and the iron. As with wet blocking, leave your project to dry completely.

Steam blocking can cut down on your drying time as the fabric is not fully saturated, but it can still take many hours.

PART – 2

ADVANCED STITCHES

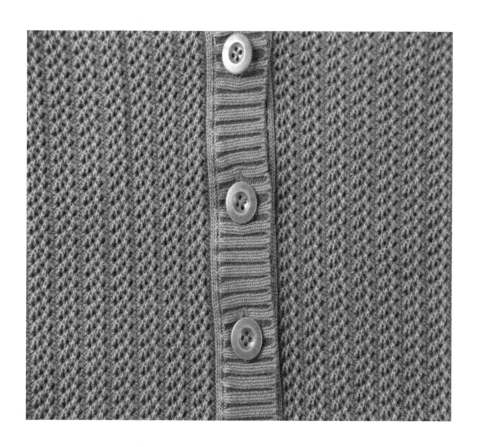

HOW TO READ A KNITTING CHART

Remember the one time that you found the perfect pattern and couldn't wait to get started and somehow cosmically even had yarn for it already only to find out it wasn't a pattern at all but a crazy graph with no instructions? Don't worry; it's not just you. They may seem impenetrable at first, but almost all charts come with their own key that makes it a cinch to work out.

Lace Chart

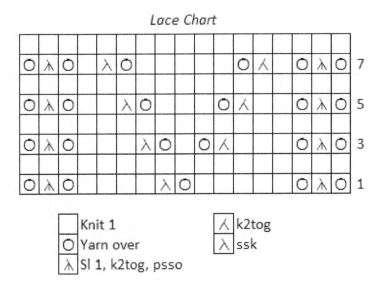

A knitting chart is simply a graphic representation of a pattern. It is a shorthand of sorts, and is often used when writing out the entire pattern would prove to be too long or tedious. It is also used frequently in lacework because the diagram can offer a good approximation of what your lace should look like. A good many expert knitters prefer working from charts as it becomes a quick and intuitive guide once you gain some familiarity.

When reading a chart, the first things to check are the key, and any chart notes. Each square represents a stitch, and these notes will explain which symbols represent which kind of stitches. You will see circles, slashes, dots, and triangles all translate to stitch techniques you are no doubt familiar with in writing (k2tog, yo, etc.).

Some stitch notation is fairly standardized-- a blank square will almost always mean knit, and bold vertical bars tend to indicate repeating the stitches framed within them. Cable turns are worked over more than one stitch so their symbols will occupy more than one box on your chart. Some pattern makers prefer their own set of symbols, however, so it is always a good idea to thoroughly check your key before moving on to the chart. It will tell you everything you need to know.

All knitting charts are written and read from right to left, bottom to top. Often the columns and rows are numbered to help keep you on track. Some charts depict only the right side of the work and have written instructions for working the wrong side. This way your chart looks more similar to how the finished piece is meant to look.

Patterns worked in the round will also only show a right side because there are no turns. Right, side-only charts will usually be numbered on the right with odd numbers only. When reading a chart where both sides are shown, work the wrong side rows from left to right. It should be easy to discern whether or not your chart shows one or both sides, but if in doubt it should certainly be included in the chart notes.

Charts are not nearly as confusing as they look, especially if you pay attention to the key and read the notes thoroughly.

Most people think they have to learn a whole new language in order to knit from a chart, but all of the information you need can be found within it!

INTRO TO STITCH PATTERNS

Now that we've gotten our construction tips down we can move on to the fun stuff. Knitting is a craft with opportunities bound only by your creativity. With such a rich wealth of history behind it (ancient socks from Egypt date to the 11th century CE!), there is already a vast library of stitch patterns at your disposal.

As you practice more of the traditional patterns you will begin to see what kind of techniques produce which kind of results, and will eventually be able to produce your own original designs! The basis of a stitch pattern is in its "stitch multiple," which is the number of stitches you have to repeat in order to complete your pattern.

In the case of a design that is worked over 6 stitches, you would cast-on any number of stitches that is divisible by 6 in order to use that pattern in your work.

Alternatively, some patterns call for a multiple plus an additional amount of stitches. If the design calls for a multiple of 6 +2, you would cast on any multiple of 6 and THEN an additional two stitches. Many more complex patterns will also have a minimum amount of rows that need to be worked in the pattern in order for the design to take its full shape. Understanding these building blocks will let you adopt any kind of stitch design to suit your purposes. This awareness is essential to transitioning from following patterns to creating them.

One thing to keep in mind when choosing a stitch pattern is how it will serve your garment. The tweed stitch you have been aching to use may be lovely, but will a stiff, moldable fabric serve your beanie project well? Each stitch pattern creates a unique looking fabric that has unique properties as well.

Ribs are stretchy, and therefore great for cuffs and hats. A seed stitch knits up thick and tight, so it may be perfect for reinforcing a sock toe or heel. Always knit up a swatch of your pattern in your desired project yarn to get a feel for how it will behave on a larger scale. Just remember your math, and you'll be able to transpose any design to any type of project.

A plain stockinette sweater can be completely transformed by the addition of an eye-catching stitch pattern, and as long as you use an acceptable stitch multiple, you can start by jazzing up your own favorite basics.

The illusory twisting cable is one of the most iconic designs in knitwear. Although it is considered an intermediate technique, the concept is fairly simple. A cable is made when a number of stitches are set aside and worked after a number of stitches that follow. The stitches pulled from work are held at either the back or the front of the piece while the other stitches are knit.

This creates either a right or left leaning twist, respectively. Often cable work is abbreviated in patterns, letting you know how many stitches should be worked and whether it is held to the front or back.

In our case, the 4 stitch cable would be written as C4B or C4F. The C is for cable (or cross), the 4 is the number of stitches the cable is worked over, and the B or F tells us if we hold the stitches to the back or the front. This crossover technique can create much more than just plaits depending on how it is used.

We're going to start with a simple 4 stitch version to get the basics down, but this is also a great cable to use for accents without overwhelming your piece. Cables like these are often worked on a purled background to make the knitted twist stand out that much more. Try increasing your cast on stitches to work a couple in a row, or decrease your purls between the cables. Find out what you like!

*just like ribbing, cables pull your fabric together, so make sure you allot for this snugness in your finished measurements.

*if you find yourself with holes on the sides of your cables, loosen up! That just means you are knitting too tightly along your turning rows.

4 STITCH CABLE

Worked in a multiple of 8 stitches, with a 4-row repeat.

C4B: slip 2 sts to CN (cable needle) and hold behind the work, k2, knit 2 sts from CN.

C4F: slip 2 sts from left needle to CN and hold in front of the work, k2, knit 2 sts from CN.

Row 1 (WS): *k4, p4; repeat from * to last 4 sts, k4.

Row 2 (RS): *p4, k4; repeat from * to last 4 sts, p4.

Row 3: *k4, p4; repeat from * to last 4 sts, k4.

Row 4 (turning row): p4, C4B, p4, C4F, p4.

Repeat these 4 rows.

DOUBLE BRAIDED CABLE

This double-cross covers a lot more ground than our 4 stitch cable. It is also written in a slightly different notation to give you a feel for some of the variations that come with the cable technique. The acronyms may be different, but the concept is the same!

Worked over a multiple of 22 sts, with a 26-row repeat.

Row 1: p2, k2, p3, k2, p4, k2, p3, k2, p2.

Row 2 and all even number rows: Knit the knit stitches and purl the purl stitches.

Row 3: p2, k2, p3, k2, p4, k2, p3, k2, p2.

Row 5: p2, (2/1LPC, p2) twice, (2/1RPC, p2) twice.

Row 7: p3, 2/1LPC, p2, 2/1LPC, 2/1RPC, p2, 2/1RPC, p3.

Row 9: p4, 2/1LPC, p2, 2/2RC, p2, 2/1RPC, p4.

Row 11: p5, (2/1LPC, 2/1RPC) twice, p5.

Row 13: p6, 2/2LC, p2, 2/2LC, p6.

Row 15: p5, (2/1RPC, 2/1LPC) twice, p5.

Row 17: p4, 2/1RPC, p2, 2/2RC, p2, 2/1LPC, p4.

Row 19: p3, 2/1RPC, p2, 2/1RPC, 2/1LPC, p2, 2/1LPC, p3.

Row 21: p2, (2/1RPC, p2) twice, (2/1LPC, p2) twice.

Row 23: p2, k2, p3, k2, p4, k2, p3, k2, p2.

Row 25: p2, k2, p3, k2, p4, k2, p3, k2, p2.

Repeat rows 1 to 26.

ABBREVIATIONS:

2/2 LC (Left Cross): slip 2 sts to CN and hold in front, k2, k2 sts from CN.

2/2 RC (Right Cross): slip 2 sts to CN and hold in back, k2, k2 sts from CN.

2/1 LPC (Left Purl Cross): slip 2 sts to CN and hold in front, p1, k2 sts from CN.

2/1 RPC (Right Purl Cross): slip 1 st to CN and hold in back, k2, p1 sts from CN.

HONEYCOMB

A very cool textural pattern. The cable twists here open and close dimples by mirroring themselves.

Worked in a multiple of 8 stitches, with an 8-row repeat

C4B: slip 2 sts to CN and hold in back, knit 2, then knit 2 from CN

C4F: slip 2 sts to CN and hold in front, knit 2, then knit 2 from CN

Row 1 (RS): Knit.

Row 2: Purl.

Row 3: * C4B, C4F; repeat from * to end.

Row 4: Purl.

Row 5: Knit.

Row 6: Purl.

Row 7: * C4F, C4B; repeat from * to end.

Row 8: Purl.

Repeat rows 1 to 8.

Brioche knits are really neat because they form a double layer of knitting. Super cozy and stretchy. An absolute classic sweater stitch.

Worked over an even number of stitches, with a 1-row repeat.

K1b: Knit 1 in the row below (insert right needle through the center of the stitch in the row below and knit, slipping st above off left needle at the same time)

P1b: Purl 1 in the row below (insert right needle through the center of the stitch in the row below and purl, slipping st above off left needle at the same time)

Knit version:

Set-up Row: Knit all sts.

Pattern Row: * k1, k1b; repeat from * to end.

Repeat Pattern Row until the desired length is reached.

PURL VERSION

Set-up Row: Purl all sts.

Pattern Row: * p1, p1b; repeat from * to end.

Repeat Pattern Row until the desired length is reached.

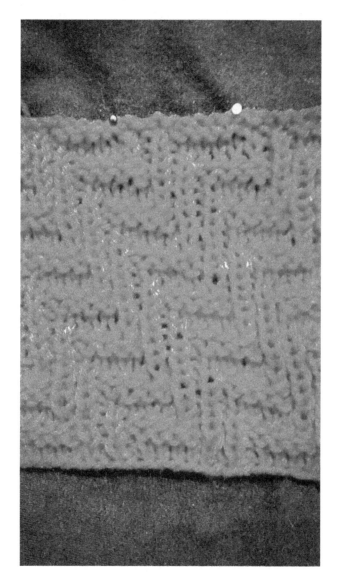

Fun, reversible zigzag with a good bit of 4 way stretch.

Very lovely with smaller yarns and needles.

Worked over a multiple of 8 stitches, with a 16-row repeat.

Row 1 (RS): * k1, p1, k1, p5; rep from * to end.

Row 2 and all wrong side rows: Knit the knit sts and purl the purl sts as they face you.

Row 3: k1, p1, * k5, p1, k1, p1; rep from * to last 6 sts, k5, p1.

Row 5: k1, * p5, k1, p1, k1; rep from * to last 7 sts, p5, k1, p1.

Row 7: * k5, p1, k1, p1; rep from * to end.

Row 9: p4, * k1, p1, k1, p5; rep from * to last 4 sts, (k1, p1) twice.

Row 11: k3, * p1, k1, p1, k5; rep from * to last 5 sts, p1, k1, p1, k2.

Row 13: p2, * k1, p1, k1, p5; rep from * to last 6 sts, k1, p1, k1, p3.

Row 15: k1, * p1, k1, p1, k5; rep from * to last 7 sts, p1, k1, p1, k4.

Row 16: Knit the knit sts and purl the purl sts as they face you.

Repeat rows 1 to 16 until the desired length is reached.

Slip Stitch Faux Rib

Not really a rib in property as much as appearance. The slipped stitches give vertical dimension to the fabric, but a lack of right side purls makes it no stretchier than stockinette. Subtle and versatile.

Worked over a multiple of 4 sts + 3, with a 2-row repeat.

Sl: slip stitch knitwise

Row 1 (RS): k1, *sl 1, k3; rep from *, end sl 1, k1.
Row 2: Purl.
Repeat rows 1 and 2 until the desired length is reached.

LACE AND OPENWORK

ZIG ZAG LACE

Eyelets soften the left and right turns of this
unconventional stitch. Its movement is great for shawls

and other flowing projects. Very delicate in a fingering weight yarn.

Worked over a multiple of 5 + 4 stitches, with a 16-row repeat.

K2tog: knit 2 together

Yo: yarn over

Ssk: slip, slip, knit

Skpo: slip one, knit one, pass the slipped stitch over the knitted stitch

Row 1 (RS): k1, yo, * ssk, k3, yo; repeat from * to last 3 sts, skpo, k1.

Row 2 and all wrong side row: Purl all sts.

Row 3: k2, * ssk, k2, yo, k1; repeat from * to last 2 sts, k2.

Row 5: k2, * ssk, k1, yo, k2; repeat from * to last 2 sts, k2.

Row 7: k2, * ssk, yo, k3; repeat from * to last 2 sts, k2.

Row 9: k1, k2tog, * yo, k3, k2tog; repeat from * to last st, yo, k1.

Row 11: k2, * k1, yo, k2, k2tog; repeat from * to last 2 sts, k2.

Row 13: k2, * k2, yo, k1, k2tog; repeat from * to last 2 sts, k2.

Row 15: k2, * k3, yo, k2tog; repeat from * to last 2 sts, k2.

Row 16: Purl.

LACE RIB

Worked over a multiple of 6 sts, with a 2-row repeat.

K2tog: knit 2 together

Yo: yarn over

Ssk: slip, slip, knit

Tbl: through back loop

Row 1: * k2tog, k1, 2yo, k1, ssk; repeat from * to end.

Row 2: * p3, p1 tbl, p2; repeat from * to end.

ARROW LACE

Worked over a multiple of 7 sts, with a 6-row repeat.

K2tog: knit 2 together

Yo: yarn over

Skpo: slip 1 as if to knit, knit 1, passed the slipped stitch over the knit stitch

Sl1-k2-psso: slip 1 as if to knit, knit 2 stitches, then pass the first stitch over the two knit stitches and off the needle

Row 1: (RS) * k4, yo, k3; repeat * to end.

Row 2 and wrong side rows: Purl.

Row 3: * k2, k2tog, yo, k1, yo, skpo, k1; repeat * to end.

Row 5: * k1, k2tog, yo, sl 1-k2-psso, yo, skpo; repeat * to end.

Row 6: Purl.

Repeat rows 1-6.

NOVELTY STITCHES

PEARL BRIOCHE

Worked over a multiple of 2 sts, with a 4-row repeat.

Row 1 (WS): k2, * sl 1 wyif yo, k1; repeat from * to end.

Row 2 (RS): k1, * brk 1, k1; repeat from * to last st, k1.

Row 3: k1, * sl 1 wyif yo, k1; repeat from * to last st, k1.

Row 4: k2, * brk 1, k1; repeat from * to end.

Sl 1 wyif yo: Bring working yarn to front under the needle, slip 1 stitch purlwise, bring working yarn over the top of the needle to the back. This produces a yarn over that crosses over the slipped stitch.

brk 1 (**br**ioche **k**nit 1): Knit the stitch that was slipped in the previous row together with its yarn over. Because the yarn over wasn't counted as a separate stitch on the previous row, no real decrease is made.

TRANSVERSE HERRINGBONE

Nicely dense and geometric. A favorite menswear stitch.

Worked in a multiple of 4 + 2 sts, with a 24-row repeat.

sl: slip stitch purlwise

wyif: with yarn in front

wyib: with yarn in back

Row 1 (RS): k2, * sl 2 wyif, k2; rep from * to end.

Row 2: p1, * sl 2 wyib, p2; rep from * to last st, p1.

Row 3: sl 2 wyif, * k2, sl2 wyif; rep from * to end.

Row 4: p3, * sl 2 wyib, p2; rep from * to last 3 sts, sl 2 wyib, p1.

Rows 5-12: Repeat Rows 1 to 4 twice.

Row 13: sl 2 wyif, * k2, sl2 wyif; rep from * to end.

Row 14: p1, * sl 2 wyib, p2; rep from * to last st, p1.

Row 15: k2, * sl 2 wyif, k2; rep from * to end.

Row 16: p3, * sl 2 wyib, p2; rep from * to last 3 sts, sl 2 wyib, p1.

Rows 17-24: Repeat Rows 13 to 16 twice.

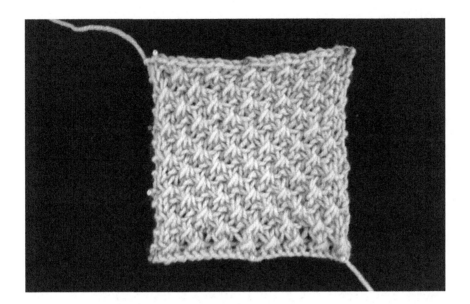

Creates a small repeating flower or starburst design. It is a neat diagonal and radial pattern and looks excellent with heavy repetition. There are many beautiful variations.

Worked over a multiple of 4 sts plus 1, with a 4-row repeat. DS (daisy stitch): p3tog, but do not let the 3 sts fall from left needle, wind yarn around right needle over the top and back to front again, then p the same 3 sts tog again and let fall from the needle.

Rows 1 and 3 (RS): Knit.
Row 2: k1, *work DS over next 3 sts, k1; rep from * to end.
Row 4: k1, p1, k1, *work DS over next 3 sts, k1; rep from *,

end p1, k1.

Repeat rows 1 to 4.

COLORWORK

STRANDED COLORWORK

Also known as "Fair Isle" knitting, named for the picturesque Scottish island where Shetland sheep have roamed for centuries, this traditional technique results in some of the most recognizable patternings in knitwear. The term "Fair Isle" is generally reserved for designs characteristic of its native Shetland Islands.

Traditional Fair Isle patterns are often small and repeating, and alternate between only two colors per row (though palettes are generally limited to around five colors for the entire piece).

Stranded colorwork involves switching between two active colors of yarn in a single row, with the color not in use being held to the back of the work until it is picked up again. This results in a loose strand of yarn behind the just made stitches (hence the name). These strands are often referred to as "floats."

This carrying technique creates a very recognizable wrong side, and the thicker fabric made by double stranding is perfect for cozy sweaters. Because these strands can be easily caught by fingers or toes in a finished garment, a single float is generally limited to 3-5 stitches.

This consideration is reflected in many Fair Isle patterns and is the main reasoning behind the expected intricacies of traditional designs.

Of course you may find yourself carrying the yarn over a greater distance, and in that case, it can be caught easily by the active color and secured along the wrong side of the piece.

1. Insert your right needle as if to knit

2. Bring your working yarn under the strand to be caught

3. Knit with your active yarn

That's it! This effectively traps the float in the space between stitches, making it invisible to the right side of the work. It is recommended that you catch your long floats every 3-5 stitches, though this can certainly vary based on the properties of your yarn or personal preferences.

Whatever measurement you decide, stick with it for the entirety of the project to ensure continuity. The most important thing to be aware of when working with stranded knitting is your gauge. Floats tend to pull the knitting together, and if carried too tightly can warp your designs and result in an uneven fit. Keep it loose!

INTARSIA

Unlike Fair Isle colorwork, the multiple yarns are not carried across the back of the work in intarsia knitting. This makes it particularly suitable for large areas of color rather than small, repeating designs. The different colors are separated into smaller balls or onto bobbins depending on how many times it is needed across the row. Each area of color is then worked from its own strand or bobbin that is dropped to the wrong side of the work when not in use.

Intarsia is generally worked in stockinette but feel free to experiment with other textures-- because this technique doesn't involve floats, the finished piece will retain all of the qualities of the stitch it is worked in.

Front

Back

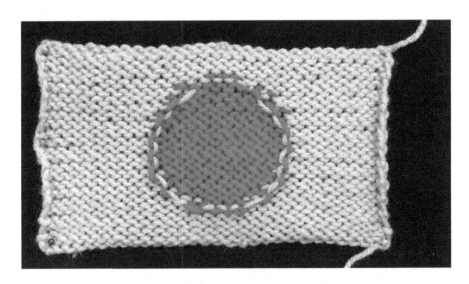

See how the stitches are not carried across the back? To
complete this circular pattern, two separate balls of blue
are needed and only one of red.

The key to intarsia work is in making a successful color change. Every time you reach a change, the old color strand is brought over the new color, and the new color is picked up from under the old color and worked from there. As the work progresses, you will see how this links the two strands together along the wrong side. This overlap makes sure the new strand catches the old one and prevents a gap from forming between the two colors.

1. Reach your color change; in this case, our MC is blue, and our CC is red

2. Bring the CC under the MC strand you were just working with

3. Now bring the CC back over the MC to begin working on your new color

4. See how the red working strand has made a loop around the blue? This catch will make sure your color changes are continuous and structurally sound.

SLIP-STITCH KNITTING

Perhaps the least well-known colorwork technique, slip-stitch knitting is actually one of the easiest because it involves only one active color at a time. The "wrong" colored stitches are slipped to the other needle and worked on the next turn.

It might help to think of it as working half a row, switching colors, and then working the other half. This method is also known as "mosaic knitting," a term coined by knitting expert Barbara Walker in the 1960s.

It is a great place to begin if you have been thinking about working with colors but are still intimidated by multi-stranded methods. It is also a great opportunity to get attuned to reading charts, as most slip-stitch patterns are written out this way.

It can be knit flat or in the round and produces a lighter weight fabric than other stranded colorworking. Below is a sample chart. The dark stitches will be slipped when working the white squares, and vice versa.

*If this is your first time reading a knitting chart, just know that charts are worked right to the left, bottom to top. We will get into the nitty gritty later in this guide. The unique part of slip-stitch knitting charts is that every row will be worked twice, with the even rows picking up the stitches you slipped on the odds and vice versa (that is why each pattern row is numbered two times when it really only makes one row of fabric!).

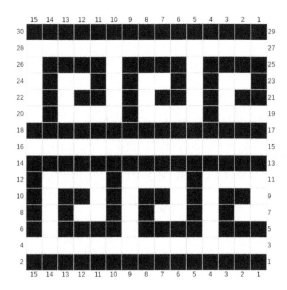

DUPLICATE STITCH

A simple colorwork technique that involves embroidering over completed stockinette fabric. Great for simple designs, afterthoughts, or people more comfortable working with one yarn at a time. Every knitted stitch is a chevron with a point at the top or bottom (depending on how you look at it), an "A" or "V" shape if you will. Consider whether you will be following an upward or downward point before you begin (for consistency) but the technique is much the same. It can be helpful to mark your design out before starting in order to keep yourself on track. Freestyle is also always acceptable!

For "A" shaped stitches:

1. Bring your needle through the top point of the A you intend to duplicate. Leave a tail of yarn at the back of the work for weaving in later.

2. Slide the needle behind both of the prongs of the A stitch BELOW your stitch

3. Insert your needle in the same place it began to finish the stitch.

4. Begin the next stitch by exiting your needle through its top point.

For "V" shaped stitches:

1. Bring your needle through the bottom point of the V you intend to duplicate. Leave a tail of yarn at the back of the work for weaving in later.
2. Slide the needle behind both prongs of the V stitch ABOVE your stitch
3. Insert your needle in the same place it began to finish the stitch.
4. Begin the next stitch by exiting your needle through its bottom point

Easy, right? Because it is literally a duplicate stitch, this colorwork will add a double thickness to whatever it is applied to. Make sure to choose a working yarn that will adequately cover the existing stitches.

EXTRAS

BUTTONHOLES

The type of buttonhole you create will depend on a variety of factors-- what kind of garment is it, how will it be worn, what size is the yarn, are there buttons or toggles, etc. If at all possible, buy your buttons before you make your buttonhole. You will then have the chance to knit a sample and make sure they are the correct size. A buttonhole should be just big enough to slip over the button.

Flat buttons will need a smaller sized hole than ones with raised heads of the same diameter. This is an important step to take because of the way knitted fabric can stretch and unfasten itself if too loose.

*Remember with buttonholes that when you bind off stitches, you must cast on new ones to replace them (usually on the next row). Yarn overs must always be offset by decreases.

*If you find yourself needing to make buttonholes from very fine or delicate yarn, try working it with a matching color sewing thread held against your yarn. This will give the hole more durability and structure.

ONE-ROW BUTTONHOLE

This creates a clean horizontal hole of variable size (depending on your needs) with average durability. Appropriate for most knitwear buttons. If you want to change the length of this opening, simply add or decrease the number of bind off and cast on stitches by the same amount.

1. Work to where you want your hole. Bring the yarn to the front and slip one stitch purlwise.

2. Bring working yarn to the back and leave it there. Slip one stitch knitwise from the left needle. Pass the first slipped stitch over it. Repeat this three times more. Slip the last bound off stitch to the left needle and turn your work.

3. Insert your right needle between the first and second stitches.

4. Draw a loop of your working yarn between the two.

5. Place that loop up on to the left needle. Repeat four more times. Turn your work.

6. With the yarn in back, slip the first stitch from the left needle to the right.

7. Pass the extra cast on over that stitch to close the buttonhole. Work the rest of your row as you would normally.

ONE-STITCH EYELET

Very small buttonholes are well suited to equally small buttons or children's clothing.

1. Work to where you want your hole. Knit 2 together, yarn over. Finish row.

2. Work the yarn over as you would a normal stitch. Finish row.

TWO-STITCH EYELET

A tad bigger than the one-stitch, this buttonhole is perfect for small novelty buttons that might have a taller or oddly shaped profile. Just as easy!

1. Work to where you want your hole. Knit 2 together, yarn over twice, ssk. Finish row.

2. Work until you reach your yarn overs. Purl into the first yarn over and then purl into the back of the second yarn over. Finish row.

Dress up any basic hat with the perfect accessory! Super cute and especially fun for kids. Pom pom makers come in a variety of sizes and are available at pretty much any craft store. Many people prefer them for their ease of use and perfectly circular results, but if you have an old pizza box lying around you're just as good to go!

1. Cut out a rectangular piece of cardboard as wide as you want your pom pom to be.

2. Cut a notch into the middle of the piece, going about ⅔ of the way down.

3. Wrap your yarn of choice continuously around the forked side. How many you make will depend on your yarn weight. It is better to err on the side of excess in the case of pom poms, since the more wraps you make, the denser and more plush your pom pom will be.

4. Cut your yarn. Thread a short piece through the notch in your cardboard and tie it tightly around the wrapped yarn.

5. Cut the loops made on either side of the cardboard.

6. Trim the pom pom to a nice even shape.

7. Fluff and you are done!

*In order to attach pom poms to different projects, just sew them on with scrap yarn, going through the center of the pom pom and back.

Another accessory used mainly for hats, although the I-cord can also be stitched onto a finished edge as a thicker, tidy border. You will need two double pointed needles or two straight needles for this technique.

For straight needles: The method is much the same, except that you won't be able to slide your stitches to the other end of the needle upon turning. Instead, just slip them over to the unused needle and knit from there. Your working yarn will be towards the back of your needle.

For double pointed needles:

1. Cast on 3 stitches.

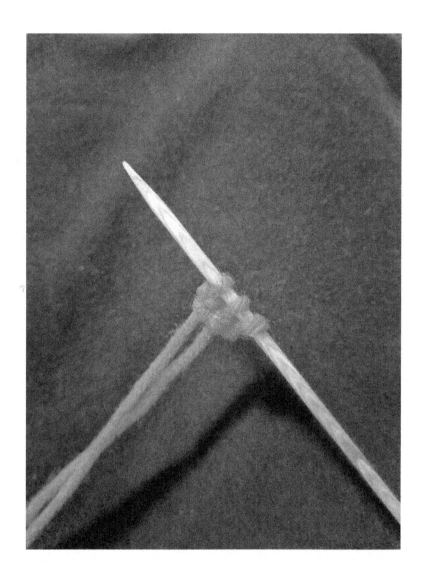

2. Knit.

3. Slide the stitches to the opposite end of the needle. Begin to knit, pulling the working yarn tightly across the back of the stitches.

4. Repeat steps 2 to 3 until the desired length is reached.

Bind off normally. Make sure to pull on the cord between turning to snug up the stitches.

LAST WORDS

Hopefully, in this book, I was able to give you a good general overview of what is involved in the advanced knitting projects. Remember to follow the directions I provided accurately and practice a few times, it takes very little effort, but you will master these techniques in no time. Once you master them, you will be ready to take on any and all complex knitting project like a pro.

I wanted to thank you for buying my book; I am neither a professional writer nor an author, but rather a person who always had the passion for knitting. I have taught knitting in three vocational schools for over 30 years. In this book, I wanted to share my knowledge with you, as I know there are many people who share the same passion and drive as I do. So, this book is entirely dedicated to YOU, my readers.

Despite my best effort to make this book error free, if you happen to find any errors, I want to ask for your forgiveness ahead of time.

Just remember, my writing skills may not be best, but the knowledge I share here is pure and honest.

If you thought I added some value and shared some valuable information that you can use, please take a minute and post a review on wherever you bought this book from. This will mean the world to me. Thank you so much!!

Lastly, I wanted to thank my dear friend Laura for all her help and support throughout this book, without her, this book would not have been possible.

Thank you, happy Knitting folks!

Made in United States
North Haven, CT
05 December 2021

12015186R00085